FALLING OFF
THE MOUNTAIN

Kalikiano Kalei

*More puerile poetic reflections on the life
experience of a young Homo sapiens*

AEOLIAN FLIGHTS | SACRAMENTO

Kalikiano Kalei/Aeolian Flights Press
5960 S Land Park Drive Nr. 256
Sacramento, CA 96822-3313 USA
http://webs.lanset.com/aeolusaero

Publisher's Note: This is a work of allegorical hyperbole. Names, characters, places, and fantasies are a product of the author's imagination. Locales and public names are sometimes used for atmospheric purposes. Any resemblance to actual people, living or dead, or to businesses, companies, events, institutions, or locales is very possibly intentional, but who can be entirely sure?

Book Layout © 2017 BookDesignTemplates.com

Falling Off the Mountain / Kalikiano Kalei. -- 1st ed.
ISBN 978-0-692-93819-5

Dedicated to all the lovely ladies (including J.) who filled my fantasies and soothed my fevered brow as a young climbing putz, in the 70s.

"...just the bare bones of a name, all rock and ice and storm and abyss. A mountain makes no attempt to sound human. It is atoms and stars. It has the nakedness of the world before the first man – or of the cindered planet after the last"

–FOSCO MARAINI

J., who nearly DID fall off the mountain, coming
down the Matterhorn Glacier in 1972.

SUMARIAN ODORS, LINGERING...

It is fitting, only to the passage of schools
Of fish, flustered, madly seeking release
In eddying pools, along the drying summer
Rogue,
Currents ignore the occasional baited line,
Floating lured wickedly on sparkling water
Towards the clutching, grasping sea.
Fluidic in release, obeying no man,
The course of river motion laughs,
Mirroring our poor human lives,
Replete with soaring aspiration
That some ultimate, everlasting memory
Will somehow survive our passing.
It is, of course, a futile, empty hope,
Since the Universe remembers no man
Nor long mourns his passage.
The substance of dreams then
Fades to total dissolution,
Fragmental human hope
That transmutes
The final diaspora
Of fateful destiny
Into the eternal
Sleep that
Follows.

RICHARD BRAUTIGAN'S CONDOMS: A DREAM OF DEATH AND RESURRECTION

Dick preferred to sheath his Richard
In ordinary *Trojans.*
Not the fancy Ribbed-Ticklers
Or purple Super-Lubes,
but regular K-Y slippery
Little Latex willy beanies
That are shaft-fitted securely
So's not to slip off amidst
Overheated mid-orgasmic lust.
Very recently a sealed pack
Of Plain-Jane Trojans was found,
Hidden for 33 dusty years
In a Bolinas floor crack
At 6 Terrace Avenue
By the present owners
Of that ghostly haunted house
Above the Pacific's lapping waves.
It sold on auction to a Tokyo collector
For 60,500 Yankee Dollars.
They were new and unused.
Sperm-filled, spent with DNA,
they would have been priceless.
An accident of unbirth
Or a sequel to *'The Abortion?'*

On the third day he rose again.
Welcome to iconoclastic
Priapistic, new & improved
America!

LAST THOUGHTS: *NOT*

Ernest Hemingway
"It is a good gun, an honest gun..."

Richard Brautigan
"Lead can be toxic..."

Hunter S. Thompson
"Only Jesus can taste this and live..."

Frida Kahlo
"The highbrows still aren't right..."

Vincent van Gough
"My own 'Starry Knight' perhaps..."

Yukio Mishima
"I'll miss my Starfighter..."

Iris Chang
"Mother will disapprove..."

Abbie Hoffman
"Steal this death..."

Jerzi Kosinski
"A truly kozmic blowjob..."

Phil Ochs
"I ain't marchin' anymore..."

Lew Welch
"Bears? Out here!?"

Ann Sexton
"I never liked automobiles..."

Franz Kafka
"Death by breath, how fitting, cough..."

AN ENCOUNTER WITH CYCLE GRRRRRYL

The blur of red and black, a streak of motion on wheels,
I saw it in my rear-view long before it drew up alongside
To reveal a perfect vision of dark-haired vital health seated
On an expensive blue, carbon-fiber roadbike.

I was making a good 24 mph, despite the headwind,
Fancying myself to be this paragon of pure, pumping energy
That few could or would overtake on a searing summer day,
Ego stroked, *macho to da max*, superbiker me!

What a shock, therefore, to my Armstrong self to see
Glistening teeth, grinning, looking positively *carnivorous*,
Framed by a bicycle helmet on the woman's lovely head
As she nonchalantly pedaled at my furious pace

Before I could collect my wits to utter a single word,
This graceful *Cheshire Catwoman* flashed another big grin

And cut in the afterburner, accelerating well
past Mach
To dash on ahead and completely out of
sight.

Aphrodite on two wheels, or
merely *Diana* on her way
To claim another victim? All I can recall are
those two
Firmly toned thighs breaking into overdrive
and leaving
Me in stupefied bemusement, sedately going
24!

Sadly, no names passed between us and I've
never seen her again.
Life is like that, though, isn't it? A series of
fleeting glimpses
Of some impossible dream is all that one is
usually left with.
Damn! Wish I knew
who that
Cycle Grrrrryl
was!

SOMEWHERE IN MY SLEEP

Tapping,
bumping gently,
outside on the slope
ghostly images
shine in the moonlight.
I wake to hear
the snowflakes beat
upon my 5 AM tent fly,
whispering urgently
soto vocce
of the morning
coming down
the mountain amidst
arboreal specters.

MATTERHORN REDUX

The pictures I still have.
All of them, after 31 years.
You, a city goddess
Posing before the summits
Your breasts framed by pack straps,
Dark eyes sheathed behind shades.
Later, drinking hot Wyler's
Seated on a mountain boulder.
The frozen cook pots are
Filled with strangely yellow ice.
Just after mid-day,
Standing on the summit,
Still beautiful, your smile glowing,
Only *slightly* out of breath!
Then the steep descent,
Crampons on ice-filled couloir,
Out and on the glacier, roped,
Tears in your eyes and scared!
You were so amusing,
The vital, alluring goddess,
Self-conscious and apologetic
For her sweaty female scent.
All I could detect downwind
Was the heady sexual aroma
Of fragrant mountain heather
In your natural perfume!
We could have easily
Died together there, you and I,
But life, as we both know,
Is *never* perfect...

ON FINDING HER HAIR IN THE BED 4.5 MONTHS AFTER PARTING

This morning
lying in bed
and reading Chinese history,
I found a single
long, black hair
next to the chapter
marked 'The Cultural
Revolution!'
All the wealth of China!

[Written in 1983]

THE MAN IN THE PALE GRAY SUIT

It's feeding time out upon the pale green
open waters.
The ocean hovers below the squatting
fireball, waiting to consume
Its blazing orb of fire that settles reluctantly
lower,
Ever closer, nearer to the ocean's restless
watery maw.
Finally, fires quenched, Sol meets its fate
and plunges under.

Blue skies darkened, each brilliant ray
mutates burnished gold.
I head away from shore upon my board and
into the turbid murk,
Mindful of possible unseen companions in
their pale gray suits.
Doubtless silently regarding my seal-like
shape upon the surface
Not unlike a wolf views a lame deer, limping
weakly into sight

Paddling out, the mental math of odds and
statistics competes
With the physical exertion of making
headway, 'til the thought's
Cut off by straining muscles, demanding
ever greater circulation.
Waves stream in, crest, pound down as I
duck under them and roll,
Surfacing on the outer lip, sputtering and

clearing my eyes.
What are the chances that my dangling arms
and splayed out legs

Will end up as a side dish for some ancient,
primordial behemoth
That nature has spent 500,000 years quietly
perfecting, evolving
The most perfect killing machine ever to
swim the shadowed deep?
I am no gambler by inclination, least of all to
wager with the sea.

Night birds soar overhead, heading out to
fish, an echelon of pelicans,
Fly in single file, low to the water. As I break
through the outside,
Piercing beyond the staggered waves and
steaming crests, I turn,
Taking in the surrounding, darkling waters,
now left in shadowed gloom.
I am alone with the sea, all but the hissing
wave crests are still and quiet.

I know quite well it is not a wise idea to be
by myself out here,
And yet the sublime beauty of the endless,
crashing, coursing waves
Forces me to relax my guard, allay my
unreasoned anxieties...until I see
The fin that is 50 yards from me, in a trough
between the waves,
Its black scalpel of remorseless precision
slicing a fluidic groove.

Quickly, quietly, as noiselessly as barely
controlled panic will allow,
I lay down upon the board and scull for
shore, looking back at that
Hungry phantom Tiger that prowls nearby
for its next meal.
Aumakua? Or simply a mindless food
processor that cares not
what casual form its evening feeding takes? I
reach shore safely.
The sea again is empty.
Night has come as silently
as the man
in the pale
gray suit.

HEARTS AND MINDS

The shrouded figure sat
alone on the rocky slab opposite,
watching as the millions of heavenly lights
traveled in perfect silence
across the velvet depths
of boundless space.
No sound dared embarrass
the night, high upon the mountain's
shoulder.
Its overwhelming absence
now pulled at his soul
with greater force
than that of the meager flame
dying before him
drawing his chilled body to its warmth.
The silence, overwhelming, utter
and consummate,
draped even the unrespecting stars
in somber, funereal bunting
as his reflections wandered softly
to the ponderous dark presence of the
mountain opposite.
Its solitude, immense and leaden,
merged like the confluence
of two inky rivers
with the dark reservoirs
of the deep cosmos above us...
a great and flowing mantle
of accepting, stoic peace
worn with perfect
and timeless, infinite composure.

The figure smiled a cold thin smile then,
for what are the concerns
of human hearts and minds,
mere sparks in the dustbins of eternity,
in the presence of perpetual
and imperishable
infinity?

TIGER! TIGER! TIGER!

Out of that cold, clear morning,
the rays of dawn stabbing
like fire tendrils
from the rising sun
touched the wings
of a flock of crows,
wheeling like dark lumps of incense
thrown aloft by a temple priest,
in loose squadrons, low
upon the farthest edge of the island's coast,
Higher and higher,
soaring up upon the thermal wind,
flying, intoxicated by the lush sweetness
of the morning air that bathed
the still quiet of the island beneath.
Soon the thermal current died
and row after dark row
of swooping shapes
descended in a sweeping curtain
low across the pineapple field
as the cold light of early dawn
reached out to embrace the earth
with many chilled
fingers of desultory disregard.
The portent birds seemed unaware
of another flock of silver wings
behind, until the savage roar of
many aircraft engines,
unbearable in their banshee shriek,
startled them into panicked escape,
leaving their sweet fruit

to fly East toward the seaward coast
and disappear, still mindful
of the powerful giant devil
their crowing had disturbed.

HAUMEA'S RAINBOW

She passed over that water way
Of wild ocean that calls each of us
Away from life and takes us home
To the unseen Ultimate *Mother
Of All Things*, 10 long years ago.
I didn't know her then, this icon
Of courage, strength and spirit.
Years after her crossing that bar
I learned of her example, her trial,
The burden of her knowing her life
Would end too soon, too very soon.
She had a warrior's heart and mind:
Strong aloha that surely would survive,
This brave and beautiful woman!
I could not share her sadness then,
Or her pain, until well past the end,
But found myself amazed, touched
To experience the legacy she left
To all who remain behind, alone.
I think of her now with grief and love,
With inspiration too; her memory
Lingers on in all of us who recall
How, when that far shore summoned,
She departed, gracefully, lovingly,
Courageously, her journey ended
Yet also begun anew and afresh.
Left for us now are the warm memories
And the spirit of loving aloha she shared
With all who came to know her.
10 Years ago she left the shore,
to swim those unknown waters,

Becoming *Haumea's* sister
Of the ocean rainbow...

ON THE WISDOM OF ANCIENT GRANDMOTHERS

The snapshot is fading.
Obi-clad, grandmother stands
with delicate hands clasped, smiling slightly
as if the burden of knowledge that travels
kaga-borne down the path of years
yet contains occasional delights.
Her venerable dignity belies the spirit
of generations which, quick to flame
at moving mountains of sumo,
causes the family doctor
so many anxious moments.
Through her eyes *Hotei* capers,
wrapped in early morning mountain mists
of Nihon's *hara*. Ah, Grandmother,
you speak silently through the eyes of
progeny
with a twinkle that captures
the smothered fires of Earth itself.

DOCBOINK HITS A CAT (1967)

My bird sits on the ramp, ready to roll out
Just as soon as I secure my sorry ass
In the aft cockpit of 57-2545.
Today I'm merely extra cargo,
Extra weight to mess up the bird's CG
And complicate my driver's mission.

As a medical stiff,
I must get my monthly hours in,
And this time around
I've strapped on
25,000 pounds of aluminum
Hitched to 20,000 pounds of *raw thrust*.
It's a cold winter day on the Minot ramp
But my palms are sweaty.

Preflight completed,
Canopy down & locked,
I hear *"Don't touch anything, Doc!"*
And *"If we need to get out quick*
I'll say 'EJECT! EJECT! EJECT!'
If you hear the third 'EJECT'
You'll be talking to yourself

And then we're lurching
Towards the active runway.
I realise I'm already breathing
A bit too heavily
Into my rubber MBU-5/P
Oxygen mask
And my helmet weighs a ton

There's a reason why
I'm always a passenger,
Rather than a righteous
Brother of the front-seat fraternity:
My equilibrium is too fragile
To handle high-G on a
Regular basis.
And I'm a nervous flier!
Some 'hero'.

I mention this again
To my driver:
*"Don't do anything fancy,
Just nice & easy, OK?"*
I can't see the wicked grin
Spreading over his masked face
As the possibilities
Of my request dawn on him.
*"Roger that, Doc.
Nice & smooth it is!"*

Then the engine of the *Six*
Spools up, airframe shuddering
Like a wild stallion straining
At the gate, *BLAM!*
We're lit and a pissed-off mule
Has just kicked me
Square in the ass!

Once at cruise
The *Six* suddenly goes crazy,
Yanking and banking
All over the sky!
Nice & easy...sure!

"Ahhh, we musta hit some CAT, Doc."
[Translation: *"Let's get Doc sick*
And throw-up
In his oxygen mask!"]
Positive G follows negative G
In a truly sadistic display
Of how perversely us medical stiffs
Are regarded by the pilots

Fortunately, I had eaten lightly.
I only barely managed to not
Lose my cookies, despite
His twisted sense of humor.
How well I recall the look
Of surprise and disappointment
On his face
When he saw
That there was no mess
In my cockpit
For the bird's crew chief
To piss & moan about.

The next time out, I wasn't
Quite so lucky! The crew chief
Got a whole case of beer
After my flight...

SEXY EAST COAT AL LEWIS (or, MA'S UNDER THE ICE AXES, I THINK...)

I / THAT WHICH IS LOST

Somewhere, I suspect
Under the antique
Russian flying helmets,
Or perhaps it's behind the ice axes,
Ma reposes.
She disappeared for nearly 24 years,
Her whereabouts mysterious,
Coyly calling up
At regular intervals to say
Isn't it time, son,
To rehabilitate yer beloved
Spelunking, mine-exploring,
Sam Cisco based,
CCAC student of a mater,
Who came upon murderhood
Quite by accident,
The result of a V-J celebration
That went on until
Zero Wee Hours
In the foggy night?
She'd never stoop to
Resorting to such a
Run-on sentence as shamelessly herself,
Of course, being an art design
Standout from the artsy post-bohemian herd
At CCAC, across the Bay.

II / THAT WHICH IS LOST STILL LOST

I surmise that the circumstances of
Her ethereal disappearance
Had nothing at all
To do with
Sexy East Coast Al Lewis,
An old flame,
Who after all, didn't even know her.
It was more probably the result of
Some unresolved
Edible Complex,
Or mebbe a bumpy camel ride
Her mother had taken in Egypt
Back when it was still safe to
Be a Mercan Gringo female
In Mohammed land.
Anyway, Ma stayed hidden
For 24 years
Until one morning|
After staring at the line-up of
Departed furry children
Atop the bookcase
It dawned on me like a Pacific sunrise
That she probably
Deserved to be located,
Despite her having abandoned
Her only progenic chille
One hot Idaho summer day
When the roof of
That damned silver mine
Up near Ketchum
Collapsed on her, thus ending

A lifetime of esoterica and arcana
And leaving
That pore
bewildered orphink
Forever marooned in the
airless vacuum of
Her absent murderly luv
To ponder why.

III / A MIRACULOUS RESURRECTION

Sure enough,
Sitting near the floor
On a shelf with old rubber oxygen masks,
Squeezing out from
Behind a rare titanium alloy
Russian ice axe,
Ma suddenly appeared,
Though a mere ghost of her former seff.
Brushing off 24 years of
Accumulated dust and dog dander,
Without a word
Or a 4th dimensional glance
She took her place
Atop the shelf,
Near Sooka-dog and
A statue of Dr. I. Jones
Of Marshall College,
Who probably didn't
Do half the things
Ma had
In her very real life of
Adventure. I think she would
Like the view from up there

And the protective comradeship
Of her adjacent woofy buddies
When it gets dark
And cold
At night.
Yup.

A FEW WORDS IN PRAISE OF QATS:

They don't consider expensive first edition
books chew-toys
They don't eat half-completed manuscripts
They don't hound you for tidbits at dinner
They keep your lap warm on cold winter
days
They have that look that says *"I know, I
know..."*
They don't need four walks a day.
They don't bark like a paranoid psychotic at
every passer-by
They amuse you at the oddest moments
They never fail to see the *ghost* in the room
They keep the house free of little black
crawly things.

And a few against:

You find your favorite books covered with a
smelly invisible residue
You find your expensive leather sofa is now
a scratching post
You find your bathroom smells like a
dumping ground for dead fish
You find your shoe contains an unpleasant
'surprise'
You find yourself unexpectedly a qitten
foster-father
You find every dust bunny is now a chase-
toy
You find yourself almost getting used to
hair-balls

You find them selecting your friends for you
You find your lady friend is allergic to them
You *suspect* your home has become a
qathouse.

PORTRAIT OF THE AUTIST AS A YOUNG PUTZ

Saturday's early Café del Sol
Saw him sucking espresso,
The existentialist autist
Striking a feigned Papa pose,
All khaki and paper,
Seated by the railing,
Writing deathless prose,
Where he imagined girls
Would walk by
And see him,
Falling instantly in love
With his inscrutable mind.
Life was rich
And full of promise,
Excitement lay around every
Bend in the jungle path,
If only
The right young woman
Would pass by and recognize
His indisputable genius.
It never worked, however.
Berkeley was full
Of such lonely dreamers.
Most of them
Have since died,
Old men
In soup-stained mufti,
Unfulfilled by even
A compassionate
Hand-job given

By a nurse
in the assisted
living
unit.

BAGGY PANTS

Cats creep across the garden
like shrunken tigers
garbed in cast-off
woolly trousers
10 times too large and late
the property of some
decrepit rural circus clown who,
having nearly drowned
in the waves of cosmic laughter
resulting from his pratfalls and antics,
has resolved
never again
to swim
too far
from shore.

FOR EVA (REFLECTIONS OF MT. MCKINLEY) 1972

Crusting winter tears
Soft as Eiderdown
Hard as ice axe steel
Flew wind-borne at my face
As I grinned
Out of the tent
Into the burning fire of dawn.

For at least an hour
My thoughts had flown
About the peaks
And down our col
To shout and play
With whines of joy
Among our shelter shrouds.

Inside, the other beard
Still drugged with chloral hydrate sleep
Lay still and unaware
Of my silent solo
Ascent of the day's
Yet unbegun Adventure.
It snorted once, then was still.

High above,
The towering mass
Of ice and rock Lay
fixed with an enormity
That labored the feeble
Recall of
My recent imagination.

A caress of zephyr from the peak
Smelt, I sensed, like
A moist but fragrant
Lover's kiss.

And then I was alone
Gasping into the mouth of ice above,
My eyes resisting
The sting,
Lungs screaming in celebration,
Feet beating steps
Into that wilderness of white
And mind.
Any thought removed, but
Seeing all too clearly
Another clime
Another aroma, A subtle scent heady
With human yearning.
Burnished flowers of yellow and ivory.

And then I awoke.

OF ROSE, AS SUNSET DIES AT DUSK IN DECEMBER

At dusk, the uneaten ducks gather to quack.
It is a cold evening, but without fog.
During such evenings, poets ruminate
and even ordinary mortals feel
the need to reflect
as the sun paints the walls
with dying fingers.
Melancholy officiates,
the agenda filled with disturbing
conversations
of suicidal but brilliant friends
who scorn doctoral tributes
to tune Porsches and drink $70 champagne
while contemplating a quick end;
and linguistics scholar friend Zhang
speaking imperfect English with a
thick Fujian accent: his remarkable
interest in the Chinese-American woman
(of great beauty) who stands—-frozen in
time
with the Chief of Medicine—fixed with
an eternal and open, simple joy of smile
in the photograph before him.
The shadows deepen
As, across the Bay, Mt. Tamalpais, guardian
of *Gold Mountain,*|
welcomes the stars and planets to yet
another night-time sky,
Something Basho said
from 17th century collections

surfaces again, to wit *"...but if I tell you*
who I am, you may not like who I am,
and it is all that I have."

Basho was no fool,
despite the antics he shared with Han Shan.
I cannot hate myself for self-indulgent
reflections of the solar fire
which mirrors on the glass of both the
window
of the room
and the crystal of my recalled sensations
with the one who forgets me
all too easily. I am too human,
and the presence of you in my room is still
too strong to erase from memory
the painful hope
of each now-dissipated day
in the progressions
of my life.
The wine warms the chill evening air...
the bamboo and pine (*sho, chuku, bai...*)
which guard the door, nod in the Eastwind
breeze.
It has travelled many thousands of miles
from Canton to stir the island trees
which lie behind the Golden Gate
before it blows so harshly
through my heart....

Just as the deadly wind
which swept from the frozen Chinese
plateau

must have filled the thoughts
of Yasuo Kato,
the first conqueror of *Qomolangma Feng* in
Winter,
as his body became ice at one
with Kobayashi, his fallen companion,
Just below the unforgiving summit.
In Yamayo prefecture
there may be crying at this moment
a woman who once knew Kato
though briefly,
only to forget too soon, that,
the *No* flute, too,
is played as if it also,
were forgotten for long stretches.

Aiiya!

Final words drift
across the Rock Band of the Chinese
Approach:
In the snow softly drifting, hot cheeks
burled: love, for me.
And so it is, as with the scripts that
people write, the walk-on actor

pauses backstage
as the play goes on about him,
the music rising in crescendos like Tsunami,
like Brahms gone berserk,
a crazed Fohn rushing down the slopes
without divine purpose.
A Joke, if you will,
of Ill-considered import ,

to engulf in avalanche of emotive
reconstruction,
the feeble ebb and flow
of mortal groping
in this darkened world.
And still the crimson pale
hangs on above, painting on the walls,
real-time ancestral memories
of 270 BO
and thoughts, expressive of the human
condition
which timeless, never die,
but are never new:

*"The woman I saw, the woman I wanted this
way; The woman I saw, the woman I wanted
that way, is here at the banquet, sitting before
my eyes, sitting at my side."*

It is not so strange, this retrospect, for did
not no less a person than e.e.cummings
himself say,

*"...your slightest look easily will enclose me
through I have closed myself as fingers, you
open always petal by petal myself as Spring
opens (touching skillfully, mysteriously) her
first rose...?"*

How poignant to hear Zhang wisely
pronounce the fact
of your Chinese heart
and your American behavior,

and my American heart
and my Chinese behavior.
It is truthfully the plotline upon which hangs
a limited option to produce
plays of human derivation
and lasting memories of a sometime liaison
with a woman of iron spirit
in silken raiment
who lingers in the confluence
of mortal rivers,
like the shimmer of golden color
that sweeps men
from the sane realities of normative conduct
to fish forever In the eddies
of romantic fancy.
Of Robert's desire to die in the seat
of his Porsche, clutching his *Chateau Moet
Chandon Dom Perignon,*
"fut!" and nothing more, limited as it is
by the myopic producer of his play...my
pity, also,
but limited.
The crimson tint of the evening
turns burnt-blood brown
till night lays claim upon all, yet again,
but unresolved,
the shimmering image of your fragile, yet
alloyed
and steely beauty.
I foreswear all further thoughts of stoicism,
and will carry
your fragrance upon
each of my evening breezes

free of constraint
and guilt-ridden /recrimination
just as in the
first bloom of Spring
and with
the last *Rose of Summer*...

LISTEN TO THE QUIET

Listen to the quiet
as it strokes the cat-like fog.
Gray shapes of dampness darting
with joyful, silent quietude,
like the ghost of a faithful dog.
A scent of pine pervades the breeze,
that drifts in from that sea,
to still the weary, restless mind
and set the spirit free.

THE SILENCE OF THE LIMBS

Boughs heavy with moisture
hang in weighty clumps of green.
On the slick flanks of coastal firs
flecks of wispy Spanish Moss quiver
as sheets of sea fog flit playfully,
capriciously undecided whether or not
to fulfill their endless, ancient pact
with the dense headland forests
as agents of life's renewal.
Dancing tendrils of the moss
pause before accepting the
invisible invitation to pirouette
offered by leering, randy gusts
impatient on their way
to caress the hot soil
that passionately awaits
their coital anointment.

IF WOMEN HAD UDDERS...

If women had udders
And cows had breasts
Would it give me the shudders
At beauty contests

Would I ogle the cows
Out standing in fields?
Would I grin and carouse
Mouthing bovine appeals

And think of the bras
That would have to be made!
(But hold your applause...
My point seems to have strayed!

If this all seems bizarre
And sounds quite unreal,
Still the thought from afar
Has a certain appeal

But it's all a big joke,
Not to worry one bit!
Since I'd likely just choke
On that abundance of tit!

FIVE UP, ONE DOWN

Wassup wit speed?
Youthful flames with white hot tongues
Still flicker out to stroke erogenous
memories of days long gone
When passions flared and dared to
accelerate life to limits unknown,
Now lost beyond recall that assumes
insanely wheeled vehicular
Velocities down recondite pathways
towards mature boredom.
Age brings forbearance, tempered by fear,
now that
Recollections of motorised
hormonal impulse fade,
Oddly muted by the squeak of bones and
failed
Cortex.

The universal male drama:
Every living act aimed at recapturing that
Which once passed, can no longer be
regained,
No vibrating echo of perfect physical energy
unleashed
By two-wheeled constructs of energy-fed
metalized emotion.
Looking back into the dim past of
hippocampic neural connections
I vaguely perceive a one-time urgency to
feed this beloved monster
Whose name may only be uttered in loudest

tones of shrieking protest,
Ridden on the cushioned spine of
motorcycled thunder.

What was it Aristotle once observed?
When asked how it felt in the darkling
twilight of human life,
To now be denied the passionate pursuits
and erotic entanglements
That immature forms of life carry as
ineluctable, burdensome baggage on
The lightspeed journey that is unfettered
youth? A relief, that ancient august
Person noted, so we are told, to finally
dismount the raging, snorting stallion
And stable it in some pleasantly
remembered, quiet pasture to graze,
Now no stranger itself to rheumy
dysconnectivities of ironic life.

One such stallion sits in my garage.
A monster on two wheels that can reach 60
miles an hour in 2.9 seconds.
Its mad, inertial doom arrested only by my
failure to wake it one last time
To ignite great explosions of psychological
defiance amid the burnt cinders
Of my own decelerating life, it sits there
patiently lurking, malevolently plotting
My ultimate end, a cataclysmic death-wish
in the making. All I need do
Is sit upon its saddle, turn the key and stroke
it from its slumbers.

Who knows but death may be a better lover
in this fatally erotic form?

A coital moment, 2.9 seconds from infinity,
beckons.

SIX SHORT CLIMBING LIMERICKS

Oh! You're such a TOOL!

There once was a climber named Jack
Who had quite an array on his rack.
In addition to bolts, he had nuts and some
'Dolts',
To fill out his climbing rucksack.

Crack of Doom!

My girl's not a climber, alas,
But she does have this cute little ass.
So although I may fall, I'm not scared at all,
When I plunge into that yawning crevasse.

But I never inhaled!

While climbing once on a steep slope
A friend stopped to blow some good dope.
As he abseiled down, he had quite a frown,
When he rappelled off the end of the rope!

In Memoriam:
Rangefinder Rick, USNPS

Here's a toast to Rangefinder Rick,
That nasty Yosemite prick!
May his 'Smokey' hat wilt, as he drives at full
tilt
To warn us off climbing *'Big Dick'*.

Lookie Up There, Mommy!

On a difficult wall one hot day
My rope-mate called out for belay,
For he'd drunk himself silly, so out came his willy,
To indulge in a glorious spray...

First Ascent of Broad Peak!

Of the peaks I have climbed in my life,
The most wondrous belong to my wife.
The traverse down below is languid and slow
But the hand-holds are wide-spread and rife!

SAINTED MOTHER TERESA, SHE IS NOT!

Mother Teresa, pray for those of us who lack your simple-minded courage in choosing to believe that there is greater meaning to human life than eating, drinking, fucking, and glorifying the self, for those of us who cannot ignore reminders about us that life is full of savagery, killing, rape, and brutal cruelty.

Mother Teresa, forgive us for breaking faith with your beautiful vision of some higher calling, great and more glorious, as millions of our kind daily dance the gavotte of death and disease, to the accompaniment of universal hollow laughter and howls of ignorant, unfed, unwashed, and benighted masses of our fellows.

Mother Teresa, smile upon our sacrilege as we seek out a less confounding, simple fairness and compromise that allows a balance of all that is a part of us; an equilibrium that assumes that although lost, all of us, there is no higher state of being found than enduring regard for our collective drama of the damned.

Mother Teresa, pray also for your little lost lamb, who although a subscriber to your faith, deeply needs more realistic, worldly knowledge of the noisome forces arrayed about her in this fouled travail we call life.

Pray especially for her belief in the goodness of her own spirit and let her boogie to the transcendent beat of life!

Mother Teresa, you are made from noble, if self-deluding stuff. Not so the fair little lamb who wanders through my own life seeking she knows not what. For she is made from flesh and bone, nerves and emotions, and has a heart that yearns for genuine love and understanding, yet knows not what that truly is!

Mother Teresa, pray that she recognises the ascendant truth of her own spiritual synergy, shining through all the shit and ordure of ordinary life that threaten to drown her, so that she may rise above the translucent surface of her feelings, like the sacred Ibis floats upon the swift East Wind's realm of lofty currents.

For Mother Teresa she is NOT!

SUMMIT VERSES FOR TROMBONE IN B FLAT

snow on the mountains
like a sweater
covers her breasts

marmot pellets
greet us on the summit
a sparrow laughs too

grim and bleak
mount ritter sits and grins
remembering last year

dark clouds
moving overhead
jealous guardians

the slow trip down
like melting ice cream
sugary glissades

after dinner cold;
yellow ice awaits us
in morning cook pots!

(1974)

KOTO-KAZE

Koto music soft on evening air Kami-like,
drifts over thirsty moonscape of jagged
garden shadows.
A thousand knives of blunted edge
strike the spine with each haunting chord.
A musical *Kaishaku-nin* stands just beyond
side-sight,
the shadow growing with each sakazuki
raised,
poised to strike. Yamato-kami hovers,
a wraith riding each chilling note,
Hatamoto of forgotten ages
sitting silently in the darkened
edges of the room. Waiting. Waiting.
Beyond the evening's pale, nighttime
America
rides the streets of careless ignorance.
What did Mishima say of a 'green snake'
strangling the country?
Beyond this room the snake coils even now.
Restless. Cold, unfed to the point of mortal
danger.
Kampai, but watch where your geta fall, my
friend.

THE SOUNDLESS TEMPLE BELL

It is late as Joshu's feet find the steps of the
shrine.
The Honeysuckle cuttings bring a smile to
the faces of the priests.

Ohayo gozaimasu. Gomen nasai...

They sit, swatting flies with ancient whisks
in the shadow of the great bell.
His face a calm mask, Joshu's coins tumble
into the Kanji-covered box next to them.
A single ray of sun catches his face
and glances sidelong off the mirrors of his
eyes.

*Kono aida wa arigato gozaimashita. Korewa
goteinei ni osoreirimasu.*

Together they savor the aroma
of the sweet flowers.
The languid scent mixes with the sweat
of their bodies and settles heavily in the
bronze cracks of the massive bell.
The late afternoon is heavy and humid.

*Yuutsu ni narimashita.   Hara ga tachimasu.
Honto ni fuyukaidesu.*

Hours pass, as overhead, like silken shrouds
the clouds rise, towering colossal unearthly
temples,
the smell of rain hanging in the evening air.
The older priest rises, claps his hands,

bows deeply and departs, followed in silence by the younger attendant.

Joshu is alone as the raindrops start to fall.

A, Joshusan'. Ame ga furiso desu.   Kaze ga fukimasu.

RABBIT GAZING AT FULL MOON

Waves pound the beach, each rush more
unrelenting.
Farther back, willows part and tremble with
each slashing gust.
Rabbit is confused by the raw anger of the
wind and sea.
High above, each dark and lamp-black cloud
thrusts, counters, thrusts again.
There is no peace tonight.
Rabbit cowers in the shadowed corner of
the Hachiman Temple,
heart beating wildly as each flashing bolt
violates the sky.
Exhausted, Rabbit lies and waits,
sheltered by the massive timbers
as the rain, in sheets, continues.
Hachiman, secretly bemused by a rabbit in
his
House of War, shifts his gaze towards
the sky. The anger thus focused, subsides.
Soon moonbeams punctuate the growing
stillness,
drawing Rabbit from the shelter of the eves
to wonder at the painful brightness
of the turgid, swollen luminescence of the
moon.
Peace has returned, the God of War is
satiated,
violence subsides and in the pine wood
clearing

Rabbit gazes skyward
with uncomplicated wonder.

\-
(1982)

HARA: THE FANTASY AS REALITY

We laugh, in our smug self-assured
certainty.
Truth in America plays the music of no-
flute.
What of the ultimate reality? Perception?
Television cameras justify all ends. No Gods
sit in judgment
so long as the cameras roll.
So long as one solitary soul is made aware
of an unfolding moment from a human
experience.
So long as one other human spirit views
sympathetically.
The ultimate fantasy is then
indistinguishable
from the ultimate reality.
And ignorance may crow
until the voice grows horse thereafter.
But no matter, for the moment alone is
truth.
Too far from land, a bird drops in death
to the sea and is consumed
without bias by the cosmos.
While the sea does not care,

neither does it blame.

(1983 after Barb H.'s BD at 'Juan's Place', Berkeley

POET FOR RENT

The wind is dying into blue emptiness
overhead.
Great valves and invisible gears grind just
out of sight
beyond the green hills of the horizon.
It is a free and softly yielding calm
that has descended briefly
to stand charmingly defiant
between the armies of the clouds.
The churning warfare of the void
is stunned into embarrassment
by the brashness of the sun
which dares now to interrupt
frigid battles of the Winter storms
and insinuate, with the coy and bashful
innocence of a baby's smile,
that conflict and pain are but a part
of the whole fabric of this life.
None the less important, but no less
the part than whole, it is the perfect time
to draw in fresh breath and pause,
anticipating the great green peace
which always follows the last warlike cry
of bleakest Winter.

THE ALMOST BABY

Reaching the mid-way point,
the locus of no return
on the flight path of my life
I reflect more and more
on the conditions
of the journey from
the Eagle's austere aspect.
On one such lonely transcendent soaring
I found myself surrounded
by lovely chattering
healthy Asian children,
being pulled down
the street
by their attentive mother,
like a string of
little ducklings
to a pond.
It reminded me that the nearest I
had ever come to realization
of this great mixed blessing
occurred some years ago
as the result
of a mistaken evening
spent and lost
on a feathered battleground
with a lovely
Chinese woman.
I found out later
that I was the father
of a small spark of human life
that promised a wonderful mixture

of many races
growing calmly together
in the belly of its mother.

My new-found status lasted for 6 weeks
until the concept was suppressed
in the course of an afternoon visit
to a witchdoctor of the healing arts.
Even now
I reflect upon the almost baby
that never quite was,
and wonder....

STORM BRIDGE MOONLIGHT

I.   Bamboo spring sprouts rise like a
challenge
to the quiet breeze outside my doorway,
pathfinder that it is, advance guard
to the next day's stormy confusion.
The *sake* has become a silver mirror
to reflect both fragile moonbeam slivers
and solitary evening thoughts
of previous evening respites. The lone pine
casts a long and nostalgic shadow
on my heart as I watch the bamboo bend,
each small gust through fronds
a cold chill winter wind
through my recollections,
till the shadows merge in dusky confluence.
High, high upon the deceitful nighttime
zephyr
a mournful *No* flute confesses sad secrets,
its rusty voice filled with reproach for
untold eons of neglect
and regretful misunderstanding.
Too late.
Time is left only to sing a brief
and sad refrain
of moments gone forever,
passed beyond any mortal grasp
or capture.

II.   Tomorrow the storms,
full with fury and nature's unthinking
devastation. Wind and tumult exalting,
the rain returns to pound the mere hopes
of fragile human dust
with vengeance born of
disregard for man's weak and vulnerable
pleas.

III.   Today a death,
tomorrow a love,
there seems no rhythm, no constancy,
just pragmatic blunder on the poorly
illuminated
stage of daily experience.
Last week, while reveling in wind and icy
snow,
the spirit in the skis sang a dangerous
and melancholy song along the crust
of the Sierra ridge. I listened....
and recognized a painful and lovely memory
dancing through the umbra
of the wind-swept wastes.
It was ameliorated, fortune
and faith be praised,
by distracting contrapuntal melodies
of far removed and distant
times and events...
the ever-present tide of the moment.

IV.   Then, this evening, returning home
from the sad web of loss spun

in the temple of mortality today,
my eyes fell upon the pictures conspicuous
on the *butsudan*...
The Husky dog, caught forever smiling,
as the great northern dogs are wont to do
perpetually, while by its side
the slim Asian woman leaning forever
on her hiking staff, outlined by trees
frozen on the flanks of summer hills.
It Is a self-invoked sadness
to confront these painful images
in all the perfect imagery
of their capture. A walking-on of coals,
a worrying of bites, insect-delivered
upon slender, insatiable feet.
And yet,
they continue, too important to ever
run the risk of being banished
to dark containers as mere memories
frozen on paper
by the unforgiving yet not entirely heartless
eye of the camera.

V. The rice Is nearly finished. The *sake* cup
now empty.
An evening of sweet and sour wondering
has drained them, as all
other elements of a sorrowful dream
flee quickly to oblivion with the rising of the
sun a'morn.
Perhaps sleep will be merciful,
a wooden draught of unconscious moments,
spanning two shores

In non-conductive, striding boots.....
For the worst,
and most painful demons of recollection
sow their seeds of regret
in the smallest hours of the
friendless night
when even the most hope-filled
song of morning's promise
shrivels in mid-utterance.
A prayer for dawn,
and then
an endless swim
in the seas of night...
no bridge
to greet the storms of morning...

RAW MEAT

The smoldering chunks of raw, black-
encrusted meat
lie scattered abstractly about the ground,
disturbingly protruding here and there
from beneath shattered shards of bright
metal
that were once the wings of an aircraft,
now unrecognizable with no piece larger
than several feet across.

It could be an impromptu barbeque
among the shattered trees and volcanic
ground,
held in a crazy scrap-metal yard, the steer
already
sliced into bite-sized chunks, seared
black and smoking by glowing coals, then
tossed
randomly about the area.

The landscape is bizarre,
a lunar field of utter, lifeless alien
devastation.
No recognizable unifying element to draw
it all together in sensible context,
save the smoke, the clouds of greasy roiling
smoke that hang over the violated ground
like a shroud of vapor from Hell.

Bereft of any human connectivity,
there is not even the smallest comfort to be

taken
from the black anonymity of it all,
the vast and indefinable dread smothering
all else,
as one steels the nerves for that first
encounter with a recognizable bit of human
flesh.

Worst is the terrible warning that the senses
prompt for what lies just ahead, for it comes
in the slightly sweetish scent that permeates
every molecule of air about the chaotic
setting,
violating any human ability to comprehend.
A brief hope for merciful dispensation from
ragged shock
instantly falls away, like the worst departing
nightmare
of childhood dreaming, as the immensity
of what has happened gradually sinks in.

A curious, charcoal colored parody
of a large children's doll comes into view,
with burnt stumps of anthracite instead of
hands.
Beneath the charred outer layer
pale flesh is split, revealing blood red juices,
of overly cooked meat and waves of
streaming vapor.
The stick arms grope outwards, bereft of
fingers,
screaming infinity, forever fixed and frozen,
for something may only be wondered at by

the living.

Later, much later, recovery crews depart,
some will eat their meals, hug their own children
and go to bed, sleeping a deep, untroubled narcosis
that mimics death. Others, shown more starkly
that brief and narrow thread of human life
revealed for the terrible, fragile thing
it truly is, shall toss and turn,
plagued by that ultimate, undeniable knowledge
so often concealed from us
until that last moment of life awaiting all.

The last thought lingers, as night enfolds all,
that in the morning, hopefully all will be revealed
as a vague mix of post-prandial discomfiture,
merely a terrible phantom of unfettered digestive
imagining, perhaps a fragment of incompletely cooked pizza,
dripping with gastric juices....*and smoking...?*

Then grim fact regains the upper hand, iterating
that the scenario is real, all too unshakably genuine,
having formulated itself from countless indelible

impressions, sunk deep in the subconscious
memory from moments of past experience
grappling with this terrible proof of our
mortality,
replaying over and over, like a cockpit voice
recorder tape of the mind post mortem
dialogues,
each time an aircraft carrying others like
yourself
becomes a parody of barbeque, Texas-style,
on some desolate plot of ground,
the nauseous, sickening aroma of sizzling,
raw meat rising like a vengeful wraith
in the weak light of tepid dawn
on Hell's threshold.

(written in the early 1980s)

DESERT HAIKU, FOR EWE (1991)

I.

In the King's gym
Hard work and sweat;
Her sweet scent of *roses*.

II.

Your body refuses
To hide its charms; I carefully
Pump more iron.

III.

A wise man never said
That to be wholly *moral*
Was to be all *good*.

IV.

Under the hot Riyadh sun;
The glint of water on ochre skin.
Ageless female allure.

V.

What is the sound
Of a water bug sinking?
'Sputter, glub, gurgle'.

VI.

Smooth thigh, graceful arm:
There is so much more
To it than that!

VII.

Cold water is not as good
As commonly thought
To quench raw desire.

VIIC.

Sometimes it is hard
To be in the Near East
Around such Far Eastern beauty.

VIII.

As Basho himself honestly
Pointed out, poets are notoriously
Dishonest, unless drunk.

A WARM PUPPY POME

Oh, cuddly puppy with snuffling nose,
That piddles so warmly upon my toes,
Your cuteness factor goes off the chart,
With every silent puppy fart.

I dedicate this pome to you,
My little producer of puppy-poo.
Despite your faults you make me smile
Although I slip in every pile.

For where can one find such a friend
With which to explore 'round every bend,
Who uncomplaining always is,
As long as he can sniff and whiz.

Forget the cats and kittens too,
That neatly bury their effluent goo,
They've never yet giv'n me a laff,
As much as you've managed to, by half!

LE PETITE BALLET
DE DAUGUEY DIEU

Oh sniffing, snuffling, doggie nose
In search of scented clues you goes,
With rapt attention to your task,
Your baptismal rite so apropos!

No odor sweet and pure will do,
Nor ordinary, this pile of poos;
The smell must be extraordinaire
To make the doggy bowels go loose.

From smell to smell you slowly pose,
To search for worthy things to hose,
And when just right, with hind leg lift',
The golden stream just flows and flows.

How delicate and choreographed
This canine dance upon the path,
You have, it seems, a firm resolve,
To give each flower a yellow bath.

And then, the *piece de resistance* true!
A humongous dump of *faecal* goo,
You leave that doggy mother-lode,
For someone else to say, "*Oh, PHEW!*"

LOVE WITH BILGE-PUMP

A few, it's true, can sail the blue
Of turgid, oceanic woo.

Not new, say you, concerning rue,
That might arise from such ado.

Our crew of two must bid adieu,
To part the pooping seas anew.

Or spew on through Sargasso's slough,
And wallow glumly in its goo.

THE PERFECT WAVE

Undulations of the Mother Womb
Sinuating, slithering liquid contractions
Roll towards us as we sit upon our boards,
Just beyond the shore break's outer edge.

The water warm, a placental broth,
Supports us, as forsaken creatures of the
land:
Uncertain prodigal spawn evolved through
Many patient millennial epochs.

The rhythmic sweep of steaming crests
ignores us
Rushing ponderously by to crash in frenzied
spray
Upon the pyroclastic lava of the shore that
sits
Impervious to all but the progeny of
eternity.
To sit so, floating out at sea, the smallest
mote,
The merest, smallest speck of fragile, sea-
borne matter,
Is to grasp the most rudimentary insight into
life,
That all our human fears are groundless.

The brilliant flash of hope-filled faith,
That Mother's fluidic coital, sine-like spasms
Will never end, bears us up with reckless
belief

That all Her waves are sublimely perfect.

Just at that moment coincident, it seems,
The green mountains moving under us finally
Grasp our bodies, furiously sucking us up
Towards our respective unknown destinies.

Borne high on anxious, colossal liquid towers
Rising far above translucent walls of streaming spume,
That moment of briefest immortality we seek
Occurs and ends again, but also lasts forever.

REQUIEM FOR A DEPARTED FRIEND

As if lightning had hammered twice, the bolts,
separated by many years in a *deja-vu* stroke of fleeting memory,
flashed out of the eerie stillness of the predawn desert hush.
Deep within that chill of darkest solitude, disturbing awareness
grew of something rushing towards perception at blinding speed.
Just beyond the limit of raw senses, it screamed silently
across the hushed sands at less than ten meters.
My intent search of the cold shimmer of azure sky
tracked the merest reflective glints of sun on distant silver,
caught and painted like a radar ghost in thermal waves of rising sun.
Within a single heartbeat the object grew explosively
until it filled my entire gaze, a fierce and beautiful machine
with wings of quicksilver came headlong, a wicked needle
forged in some demonic, cataclysmic fire, taking vectors
as if targeted with obdurate kinetic force toward
the unprotected human heart and mind.

Faster than thought, quicker than regret,
with hellish haste
I became caught up in vibrating sympathy
with ancient urgent forces
as the silver-winged machine screamed
wildly over my head,
engine howling and afterburner bellowing
like a demon song
gone mad with raging pain, passing so near I
felt I could
have reached up and touched it, strangely
drained of all
fears of death and daring to watch, ears
ringing, as the
aircraft lifted suddenly skyward, going
beyond the speed
of sound, soaring impossibly high into the
vast
and limitless ocean of heavy desert air.
Once again alone, left gaping, staggered by
the sudden shock
of pure vacuum in its passing, there was
very little left to affirm
what reality had just existed: the cool of the
early desert morning, the
shifting sands of experience, memory, and
emotion, the emptiness
of insubstantial fragments of time and space
gone forever.
Nothing more than this...and a single distant
flash of sun on liquid
silver wings, flaring briefly in the endless
depths of cobalt blue infinity

to remind me of what had come and gone...again and forever.

A CHINAMAN'S CHANCE

Hezekiah Chang was 15, we are told;
an honor student at McClatchy School.
His family came to the United States
from China, where his parents had been
forced to perform hard labor during the days
of the Cultural Revolution. They were both
teachers, well-educated intellectuals, yet
believers in the *One True God* of the Bible.

Mao's secular cruelty could not suppress
their faith that *Jesus* would bless them
and watch over them, as they struggled
to remain alive, despite the many terrors
that they suffered, until that moment
two decades ago, when they became
Americans in the land called *Gold Mountain*.
Hezekiah was their first-born, a strong boy!

Intelligent, handsome, a natural student,
Hezekiah excelled in math, studied piano,
volunteered after school at the hospital,
attended to his parents' wishes that he
become the proud son they had hoped for.
He would graduate, study medicine,
become a doctor, marry a Chinese girl,
in the custom of their family and ancestors.

Hezekiah was viewed by others at school
as a nerdy little yellow creep, all except
for one girl, a young Latina, also bright,
but the daughter of atheistic Chilean

socialists
and former Sandinista migrants, now
American.
Seeing in each other things denied their
peers
Hezekiah and the girl grew to value each
other,
unknown to both sets of their parents.

Last week, Hezekiah and the girl left school
to study together at the end of the day,
walking in the parking lot when shots rang
out,
reverberating off the brick walls of the
school.
The bullets of an automatic weapon caught
them both. A car sped off. A random crime.
Hezekiah died there, as did she. No one
knows
why, to this day, they were singled out.

A Chinaman's chance. *America the Beautiful!*
The next day, Hezekiah's mother was heard
to remark that it had been God's will, that
He had had some greater plan for them that
somehow transcended our human
understanding.
The girl's parents were less forgiving,
cursing
the implacable chaos of this Godless world
with all its barbarity and brutal, random
cruelty.

Somewhere, faint hollow laughter echoes,
wafting through the mind like a ghostly
breeze.
But is it Godlike, or is it human? We should
be in
no hurry to find out the answer to that
single
unanswered question, although we suspect
there is nothing to learn and no way of
knowing;
no way of making any sense of what appears
to be...a *Chinaman's chance.*

CENTURION

Age creeps up upon us all like a small gray
cat,
Stealthy in approach, with softly padded
footfalls,
Sensually, movements vague, yet with
determined
Vengefulness, sinuously stalking each man
and woman,
Mewling, purring, mercilessly pursuing,
eventually
Climbing uninvited and demanding upon
each lap.

That dark centurion of time, keeper of
infinity,
Guardian of predestined oblivion and
destruction
Visits in the darkest hours of the utter
catlike night,
Marking all without concern for beauty or
strength.
Unknowable, implacable *finity* gathering its
black shroud
Of ultimate, inescapable, darkest, wearying
exhaustion.

Once young, once strong, once pulsating
with energy
The high are brought low, the lowly elevated
to heights
Known only to some higher purpose that
transcends

Our understanding; in the final
accounting, *nothingness*.
The lonely anguish of age mercifully dulled
by fading reason,
Senilia of ineluctable dissolution and
ultimate decay.

That little gray cat is on my lap as I speak,
purring
Its obscene pleasures as it kneads my leg,
small, fatal,
Herald of impending doom, whisking its tail
to give the lie
To its irresistible deceits, deceptions of
bleakest promise.
Small gray icon of doom, it yawns as if
nothing matters.
Poised upon the brink of the centurion's
fateful whim.

MYTHOS MYSTERIOSA FEMININA

I am haunted by a soporific vision,
My days and nights, my every waking
thought
Suffusing!

The stuff of mists and ethereal vapors;
Rare and indistinct scents and half-images,
Intoxicating!

Never the same, forever changing,
Ever discharging currents electrical and
Incapacitating!

Near, almost within my outstretched reach,
But never close at hand, blurred form
furiously
Scintillating!

The phantom of these dreams
Has me in its sweat-stained, taloned
clutches,
Unresisting!

Every atom of me knows well this *familiar,*
Yet knows it not, hidden behind its
vagueness,
Inviting!

Though I sleep, it remains stridently awake,
Drawing me closer to its sinewed belly,
insanely
Feeding!

The only certain knowledge I have
Of it... its exhausting, insatiable, alluringly
savage
Mating!

OFF-HANDEDLY, HIAWATHA
By Henry ('It's a *Longfellow*') Wads-worthy

On the shores of Gitchee-goomie,
In a far-off, ancient time,
There camped a brave young warrior
Who drank himself sublime.

"Why, oh why, brave buddy",
Asked all his friends so true ,
"Do you drown yourself in alcohol,
Till it turns your red skin blue?"

"Alas", spake young Hiawatha,
In words one hardly heard,
"My dog has up and left me
And my girl thinks I'm a turd!"

On hearing this sad tale of woe,
From their Hiawatha's lips,
His warrior friends came near to him
To offer up some tips!

"First off", said one to he,
"Your dog can be replaced,
And second, more important yet,
"Minnehaha had bad taste."

"So, take fresh heart and listen up,
You've still got both your hands;
Go make a date with Rosy Palm
And exercise HER glands!"

On hearing this, the troubled buck,
Did straightway come to rue

All those who say a hand-job's not,
The same as a female screw!

In days to come, so did our lad,
With imagination's aid,
As in his mind he fantasized
That he was getting laid!

On the shores of Gitchee-goomie,
In a far-off, ancient time,
There camps a brave young warrior
Who thinks "by-hand's" just fine!

A GLINT IN LOKI'S EYE

High up in the Stygian ebony of desert skies
The stellar fires of deepest unending space
Perfuse our thoughts upon the merest
twinkle
In the stony gaze of whatever gods exist;
The murmur of voices, swept on soft
breezes,
Punctuate the darkness that surrounds us
As we drink and muse on life's eternal
drama
In benighted realms of coruscated thought.

Later, the starry skies shine blindly down,
Rejecting assignations of animistic gravity,
Pulling back from blackest insensate
emptiness
In vaporous streams from every pore of the
body.
Lovely Laidia, daughter of Loki, poses
elegantly
On the verge of eternal ancient echoes to
Occupy my thoughts as the ebb of tidal wine
Floods the desiccated lakebed of my
rumination.

Forged from icy crystal on Thor's Artic
hearth,
All vital, exotic human warmth forever
damped,
The cool desert air surrounds us, chills us,
draughts

Replacing the solar warmth that has fleetly vanished
With the appearance of the luminous full moon.
Before you left, I felt the electric spirit deflect
Upon the smooth exterior of your female armor,
A glint in the unbearably bright mirror of Loki's eye.

LEFT BRAIN,
RIGHT BRAIN,
LOWER BRAIN.

It has been fairly well established
That the ancient, prehistoric reptile
Had two discrete neural control centers:
One in the cranium and the other
Situated in the lower hind-quarters.
Both were about the size of a pea.

The theory has recently been advanced
That modern man, despite the cursed
blessing
Of his reasoning abilities, also has two brains
As well: A rather large and complicated,
Bilateral one, and a smaller but dominant
one,
More about which we shall hear shortly.

The former appears to control man's
Conscious behavior in nearly every aspect
<save one>, while the latter operates on
An autonomous, reactive basis—functionally
Best illustrated in mixed gender situations.

The lower 'nether-brain', as it is regarded,
Activates automatically in the presence of a
fair
Member of the opposite sex, instantly
rendering
All male bodily functions subject to its
Genetically programmed instructions.

I'd like to arrange a limited clinical
Demonstration of this for you, but don't
Blame me if the experiment gets somewhat
Out of control. After all, the 'nether-brain'
may
Well be in the *genes*, but it's in the *jeans*, as
well...

THE CELTIC KNOT

Yesterday you resurrected ancient wraiths
Of Celtic mist and blue shadows of the
forest.
Howling barbarian hordes descended from
The forgotten regions of my ancestral
memory
To wage furious assault upon the least
defended
Portals of my castle keep.

The air was filled with death cries of the
invader
As the strongest of my defenses crumbled
Before the irresistible force of those who do
your bid.
My strength, which matches that of pale
tigers
In the face of all other dangers, dropped
away like rain drops
Before the fiercest of your burnished
legions.

It was all to no avail and in the final clash
My heart was captured, taken prisoner,
bound
In steel chains woven from the darkest
strands
Of scented hair that wreaths the alabaster of
your fair neck.
And like a helpless prize of warring passions

forsaken
I was brought to you for judgment.

The flash of silvered metal from your lovely
ears
Told me all I needed to know the outcome
of that moment,
As the mobius knot of legend shrouded
runic myth
Pronounced the silent admonitions that all
who hear
Must fear and acknowledge fully as the
legacy
Of infinity's capricious, timeless whim.

There I swayed, poised above the fires of
loveless hope,
Held from falling to my doom by the
slenderest
Of ropes woven from that fall of darkest
moonbeams
That is the crowning legacy of your regal
beauty.
Defiantly, I scorned mercy then, searching
your eyes
For a saving evidence of the deeper feeling I
hoped to see.

Alas, they were perfect mirrors of emptiest
black space,
The void flinging back the certainty of my
futile quest.
Before that final plunge into the fiery limbo

of your soul,
I paused. The desolate refuge of the
vanquished heart,
The undervalued, cast-off armor of this
lamented battle borne,
As yet another sacrifice to that hellish Celtic
knot!

THE KITE

Out in the desert, all is quiet in the early
morning.
The sun hangs upon the horizon with
indecision,
Seemingly struck with the notion of
remaining to observe,
Forever perched upon the lip of this dusty
desert world.
Shadows are lengthened purple wraiths, yet
vague promise
Permeates the uncertainty of a new day, a
new dawn,
With renewal and resurgent thirst for life.

High above the tawny sands, the endless
ranks of dunes
That march like some great soporific silicon
army;
Pursuing an unseen and distant perimeter of
the spirit,
The azure of the sky descends from utter
cobalt depths
To cast a solar aura upon a single kite with
wings outstretched.
Soaring in endless spirals upon the cool hush
of stillness,
it is searching for a trace of warmly rising
thermal currents.

The kite has been on wing for many weary
hours,
Riding out the thickened columns of neutral

desert air
As it seeks undaunted the invisible
upwellings that will
Bear it higher into the full glory of its
elemental nature.
Watching this tableaux, the ponderous and
still undecided sun,
Appears to linger on the verge, holding back
its solar beams
As if enjoying the spectacle of the kite's
laboring efforts.

But then, subject to the unquestionable
intention
Of some universal, willful spirit that even
stars must obey,
The sun allows its rays to chase the
remaining shadows of night
Back into their caves of refuge deep within
the embarrassed earth.
Instantly the towers of air heat up, throwing
raw Brownian energy
into the massive ocean of fragrant heated air
the kite has discovered,
And with pinions spread, it wheels to meet
the freshened Eastern wind.

The desert fastness of that raptor's aerie
stretches on forever;
I fancy I am the falcon that searches for
those elusive thermal currents.
You are the lifting energy of the graceful,
warming radiance of solar heat
That inspires my instinctive flight toward

the dazzling
Illumination of your sun-like spirit's fatal
essence.
The endless desert dance of love and death
begins.

ODE TO HIGH-G FLIGHT

Pullin' Gs,
Feel the squeeze,
Brain somewhere
Below the knees.

Grunt out loud,
Slashing cloud,
Getting sick,
Not feelin' proud!

Valsalva's fine
But not divine,
Yankin' stick
An' flyn dakine!

Redout nears,
So drop the gears.
Flare and land;
Forget your fears!

Then shut 'er down,
Right on the ground,
The O-Club awaits:
A beery round!

LOVE IS A TWO-WAY STREET

Love is a two-way street.
Unfortunately, your lane is closed for
repairs
And my own leads back to a highway
Still under construction.

HARSH MOON OVER RIYADH, 1992

In the night sky, full Autumn moon
Casts shadows as I watch for rabbit
Busy pounding his rice-cakes.

No other near to share the moment
Nor another cup nearby for company;
Rabbit moon is mine alone tonight.

Full and bright, moon fills the sky
With cold and distant light, just as my
Heart is filled with muted longing.

I would be elsewhere to enjoy this
But all around is restless sand, blowing
Small storms through my thoughts.

Love for me is scattered in many mirrors,
But none are here to catch and hold
Clear moonlight reflections as I drink

Chang'e will be there to smile once more
When peace and love next fill my spirit
As the wine and moon-cakes fill me now.

Full Autumn moon over Arab desert!
How empty it feels to lack the comfort
Of soft flesh and long ebony hair tonight.

REBIRTH

The wind sweeps all before it like a scythe,
Verging as it does upon the brink of a
ruinous fall.
Below and beyond stretches a chasm of
unseen depth
Disappearing into the mists of obdurate
saline spume
That cluster hysterically, like ghosts upon a
yawning crypt.

Strangely without fear, shadows leap into
that blackest void,
Congealing flows spattering in the softest
fluidic mass
Of oceanic skin as the canyon walls close
and converge
Upon the intrusion, wave crests undulating,
seething
In the wake of molten lava spewing forth
from heated depths.

The restless seas receive the steaming seed
with eager desire
Closing upon it as it explodes into shivering
tendrils of
Flaming, chaotic magma. Orgasmic shudders
of completion
Rend the frenzied mating rituals of Earth
and Ocean
As the endless cycle of rebirth is begun
anew.

THE OCEAN'S DIALOGUE
WITH THE SEA-CAVE

'I keenly sense your empty hollows
And long to fill them with my tides,
As I would have you gentle my wild currents
And soothe my ancient alluvial longings!'

'....sssssssshhhhhhhhhhhhhh!'

FALLING OFF THE MOUNTAIN:
THE CLIMBING KOAN

You can't fall *off* a mountain.
It's not something you would notice
While clinging to that ledge up there,
But carefully consider: You really *can't!*

Where does a mountain begin?
Where does it end? At which altitude does
It start? How deep do its roots reach?
How broad is its circumference?

When we tightly close our eyes
Does any mountain cease to exist?
How far do we need to travel from it
Before we have actually left it?

When you finish climbing a route
Does the mountain disappear?
When we travel away from it,
Do we take any of it with us?

As your weary fingers peel off
The little 'nothing' holds high up
The face, as gravity makes you slip,
Are you falling off the mountain? No!

When we start toward the summit
Does the mountain take *us* with *it?*
Think hard about it; no matter how hard
You try, you can't fall *off* a mountain!

CARDIOTOMY

HX & PE:
The diagnosis was obvious from the onset, with critical action required. It began, not with minor heartburn sensations or mildly radiating pain, but with a crushing, aching, breath-taking squeeze of the emotions. One moment patient was functionally normal, unaware of difficulty, the next he was transported instantly into transcendent space. With alarming force and speed, patient experienced aberrant cardiac rhythms. Strangely, instead of going asystole, patient's heart rate accelerated wildly, raging out of control and into unmanageable extremes of sensory tachycardia. Apparent pheromonal assaults on his olfactory threshold continued collaterally. Lab results were startling, with the testosterone titer beyond normal limits; emotional enzymes were off the scale completely. The news was soon broken to the patient: he had suffered a heart seizure of the most precarious and unpredictable kind. Clearly, a strong surge of female attraction had penetrated all of the body's natural defense systems protecting his feelings and he sustained a massive, extensive (near fatal) spasm of attachment to this causative paragon of pulchritudinous passion.

IMPRESSION:
Fortunately, medical science can today perform miraculous recoveries today, but amazingly, the object of patient's precipitant affections is a *cardiotomist* (At least we think she is). At any rate, she has replaced patient's old, worn, melancholy heart with a new one that sings and smiles. Her emotional post-surg rehabilitation program is doing wonders for him, although it is noted that his cardiac rate is still tachycardic whenever she enters his room. Despite the fact that he shall never be fully recovered, and must continue to receive regular infusions of her lovely spirit and charm (most particularly plenty of physical therapy), the cardiotomy itself was brilliantly successful and the patient himself is ecstatic over his short-term chances for success!

PROGNOSIS:
Prognosis continues to be excellent! Rx: Continue treatments as ordered, review progress PRN. It will, of course, be critical to maintain spiritual and physical therapy without interruption for a full recovery!

OH, OBLOQUY!

Oddly obdurate opprobrium
Occurring ocarina-like, obstipative,
Obdurate on ombre
Orthopaedic ontologies

Oh! Omniscient omophagia,
Ordered by onomastics?
Opining opiates of oedipal origin
Occultation...or obiter-dictum?

Obviate the obconic orgasms
Of obeisance, obfuscate oral
Obligatos off obscenely
Ovarian overtures

Obnoxious obloquy!
Oscillative osculation's
Orthodoxy, osmotic, obsessive,
Ostomic in ovulation!

Ovoviperous oviposition
Opportuning oxytocic opprobrium.
Otiosistic and orotund orology
Of orgasmic, oronasal ordure...

DA WIZUDA WOIDS

Dere once wuzza Wizud
Who dabbled in woids,
He slottahed his nouns
An'e moidered his voibs.

His knowledge wuz small
Butiz bullshit wuz great
An'e moidered da language
All ovah da place!

Dis wizud blew smoke
Lik 'is pans wuz afire,
An da lengt ovis phrases
Wuzza ting ta desire.

Dat is until wun day
Wen sumwun got bright
And figgered his game out,
Thus endin' is plight!

TROTSKY GOT THE POINT: DO WE?

Objectivistic revisionism stands moot,
As recidivist socialismus rallies to establish
That Leon, that dear porcine Snowball of
Orwellian angst,
Was murderated by a blow to his frontal
lobe
Delivered from behind with penetrating
Impetus.

Three score years have passed since
Leon took the brunt of Stalin's sharp latent
criticism
Not to heart, but to brain. And now the
aesthetes argue
Over whether the instrument of deliverance
was an ice pick
Or that instrument of mountaineering
known as a climbing
Eispickel.

It is too late to axe Leon himself, poor
intellectual
Martyr that he was, for he has gone to
ground forever now,
Conjecture reigning supreme, with only
Madame Salas
Able to clarify the burning question of what
Exactly was used in Leon's premature
prefrontal
Lobotomy.

Ramon Mercader knows, but he is gone,
Somewhat after picking his chosen anti-
Menschevik target:
Lev Bronstein. Those sneaky Heebies,
forever lurking in
Ev'ry woodpile! Even a pseudonym was not
enough forethought
To save our mensch Lev the terminal
Jeebies, on that fatal
Day.

Lev got the point, but does anyone today?
Ana Alicia Salas has recently ignited a new
party schism
By declaring her intent to auction off that
infamous
Mucronated cudgel to the highest bourgeois
bidder
For serious rasbuckniks.
Sic transit Gloria
Mundi!

YOUR FASCIST HEART (FOR SOOKS)

In the darkest shades of stygian blackness
you come to me,
A wraith of cool flesh and infinite ebony
eyes, cloaked in dreams
And clad in the scent of ancient earth and
mysterious oceanic deeps.
I am seated, slumped before a guttering
candle,
Wits aflame, senses vibrating to a welling,
soundless primal scream
That resonates from deep within the heat of
my essential being.
The shimmering outline of your naked form
reaches out
to overwhelm my defenses and embrace me,
glowing in Silurian lava,
with ghostly arms that end in sinewy, steely
talons.
It is the mirrored bottle, finally, that screams
out warning,
As your presence fires the chambers of my
mind with melting heat:
I am NOT the captive of this disturbing dream,
I am the KEEPER!
Lurching to my feet, chair flung back to the
stony verge,
I advance to clutch the phantasm of my
most desired fears, as instantly
Across the room the vision cools, becoming
bluest crystalline glacial ice.
With desolate finality, an Arctic gale sweeps

my chamber,
Chilling the spot where a moment ago the
burning gates of hell yawned wide.
The frozen apparition reflected in the bottle
vanishes into tumbled mist.
Wearily, with the fatigue of approaching
death, I stumble back
From the abyss. The candle flares once and
gutters out as I lift my cup
To the wine-dark blood of your icy loins
that welcome a conflagration of oblivion.
Somewhere, just before my senses fade into
soporific limbo,
I hear the faintest hint of exquisitely muted
song...your fearful, alluring
Fascist heart is singing...*singing!*...sweetly
into the muted turmoil of my dreams.

(Riyadh, 1993)

IT'S A JUNGLE OUT THERE!

The forest trail disappears
Into a tangle of vines and undergrowth.
We pause, on the verge of the emerald
oblivion,
Before entering into this hot and steaming
Unknown place that lies before us.,
Senses alert, breathing suspended,
As the disconcerting sounds of uncertainty
Resonate in the humid air like a great,
unseen
Temple Bell of pagan sacrificial worship.
Faintly, saturating the molecules of vapor
With dangerous urgency, the sounds of
Drums vibrate on the mists of morning.
You walk ahead, I follow, guarding you
Against recollections evoked by
Those dreadful beats.
I watch your lithe body as it hesitates,
Stepping over tangled masses and heaps of
Fetid vegetation with uncertainty.
The effort soaks your clothes with sweat
And molds them to your form with primal
allure.
Ahead? Unknown emotional horizons to
navigate?
Cannibals of the mind waiting to ravage
heart and soul?
A human tiger trap awaiting but one fateful
misstep?
Be careful, dark and beautiful one, for it is
A jungle out there and love favors only the

Quick of thought and the bold of spirit.
There are many dangerous animals
Lurking in the jungle we have entered
But never forget the fact
That the most dangerous
Predator of all is man...
In the chaotic wilds of your thoughts,
I silently await my moment
To spring.

FEED THE BEAST!

Pity the nun, for she is the bride of Christ.
A purer, more sterilised love affair does not
exist,
For there can be no ardent consummation of
desire
When the husband/lover is wrought from
air & myth

Envy the hot spirited woman of flesh and
blood,
for hers is the choice between artful self-
deception
and abject sensual abandon to the ancient
curse of
insatiable pleasures of thirsty, demanding
senses.

Within each woman lies the bigeminal soul
Of purest saintly spiritual bride and lustful
fiery hellion.
Each component of this duality daily needs
to feed:
The saint on airy vapors, the carnal beast
upon raw meat.

My advice to you, having known many nuns
and an equal number of hormonally
optimised females in the course of my
journey down the Tao's water way,
Is to open the cage, unbar the door, starve
the nun...but FEED the beast!

IN THE DESERT OCEAN DEPTHS

Life without a porpoise, in a sandy inland sea,
Is like breathing seltzer water straight or mixing it with tea.
The bubbles full of CO2 can hardly help you thrive
And the thought of fizzy Earl Grey, what a horror *THAT* connives!

The waters that surround us here are very dry and deep.
They drown our spirits and swamp our souls, but through our lives they seep.
The beach itself goes on for miles and miles of sandy dunes;
The trick you see is to survive by humming looney tunes.

So pack your suntan lotion tube and grab your diving gear,
And take a dive into the depths of this water not-so-clear;
At the very least you'll see odd fish and other stranger sights,
With which to rehydrate your views and bring you back aright.

But as for swimming in the schools of desert dolphin herds,
It takes a special kind of spirit to embrace what's patently absurd

And dare to search for endless waves on
non-existent seas,
In hopes of finding coolness in the absent
ocean breeze.

At long last, after thoughtful pause and a
year of desert nights,
A silver dolphin of flashing clarity may swim
into your sights;
If it does, grab hold the porpoise offered and
ride it out to sea
For the secret of fulfilled life here is to
simply live and *BE.*

MAKING THE WIND AND THE RAIN

Wind of the Is, dance with the rain.
Drops of the rare and precious water
Fall on the dry sand, emptiness.

Wind of the Is began its trip
In the fragrant orient. In streams of air
Far above green Canadian forests
It continued its flight.

Wind of the Is shakes the sky
Above the desolation, drinking of dry sand
And refreshed with water it has created
By its thunder and light.

The sand waits patiently
For another tryst, pleasured by
The unexpected attentions of
The Wind of the Is.

[This poem generated in 1991 by my early IBM 8088 PC (really!)]

116

STONE FACES (AKU-AKU)

Do not look at me with eyes that do not see;
Think not of me with a heart that is numb.
Do not feel the searing heat of my ardor
With insulated nerves and deadened senses.
The prison that contains this heart
Is clad in granite chiseled from living rock,
Its walls reflecting the cold and stony
emotion
Of your own pent-up rage like a shattered
mirror.
As a sculptor, I bear two powerful tools
Which may break apart and utterly smash
That frozen, awful façade of silence that you
wear
With hammer blows of undeniable force.
Only the briefest spark is required
To summon the stonecutter's craft to life,
A breathing, coursing transformation
wrought
By the mallet of Yang upon Yin.
When that moment comes, be ready,
For there will be a tremor of blinding power
That instantly destroys the unseeing, useless
hate
That has locked your soul in its sheath of
living quartz.

(Rapa Nui, 1985)

PAS DE DEUX

High above the tree line stands a small ivory
flower.
Alone in all the lonely universe, the white
bloom thrives,
Surrounded by tall, brooding sentinels of
silent dark stone.
It is a quiet early morning time among the
gaunt towers;
Glacial snows glint in the mirrored surface
of icy rock faces
As the cold gilt of dawn's light gathers in the
azure sky.
Hardly a breath of rarest air stirs the petals
of the flower
As it reposes on the frigid flanks of the
sleeping mountain,
A small presence amidst the giant shadows
of the fleeing darkness.

The palpable quietude hangs frozen in time,
as icy tines
Of hidden rock-hoar which have never felt
the warmth
Seek sterile solar light in this splendid
temple of desolation.
Clinging to the silent stony cliff face,
Edelweiss, the
Noble Whiteness, grows bravely, humbly in
the company of these
Mute and stony crags, an incarnation of the
inconsequential beauty

Of all transient life in this reliquary of fire
and ice.

Then, without a herald louder than a
whisper, the wind,
That restless spirit of all that strives to exist
in the confusion
Of universal empty chaos, rushes down from
the heights
And tallest spires of granite to roar out with
unbound passion
The furiously unknowable emotions of some
nameless demon,
Filling the human heart to its depths with
awe and wonder;
The Edelweiss, greeting what we pale
mortals fear and dread,
Trembles and begins a dance of pure
abandon in the embrace
Of these Aeolian zephyrs from remotest
Arctic regions.

The flower and wind begin their timeless
pas de deux,
Satisfied with each other's company and
lacking nothing,
While far below our mortal world embarks
upon yet another day.

TEMPLE OF HEAVEN, PILLAR OF SKY...

To see you, raven-haired daughter of Han,
In whose form a quarter of the world's life
surges,
Is to tactilely experience the molten earth-
core moving,
The view the deepest submarine rifts of the
eternal oceans
Sublimely revealed in all their ancient
tectonic complexities
Before the labyrinthine gaze of merciless
infinite heavens,
To sense the promise of eternally hope-
filled human spawn
Of civilization that fate cradles within the
ancient temple
Of your exquisitely beautiful ancestral
spirits.

Essential aroma of Yin overwhelms my
senses
With the jasmine-scented universal mystery
Of your anima, a compilation of most
intoxicating
Chemistry that dares to steal the heart of an
immortal,
Let alone the vulnerable soul of this
temporal voyager.
Is it any wonder then that the merest
thought of you
Brings forth all-consuming fires of wildly
raging lava

To flood this heart, which the most
unconscious
Of your smiles may provoke to erupt?

These puerile words of adolescent ardor
Tumble unbidden from the mouth at my
peril,
For flowery spoken phrases are an empty
substitute
For truths which only the truest heart may
know.
Yet I am overcome by the aura of your
splendid
Womanliness, bemused beyond stupefaction
by the
Essence of your Yin, by the exquisitely
graceful female
Creature that you are, as the resonant
chordal syncope
Provoked in my own Chi vibrates in
sympathetic harmony
With your life force...a rhythm that falls
upon the dry Earth
Like wind before the rain.

I share the restless waves of sand you walk
upon,
The heated desert air you breathe, the
impersonal corridors
Of heartless medical science in which you
pass each sentient
Day. I am the landscape, the mechanical
panorama man

Of formular healing, capable of mending all
human hearts
Save my own! And you? You are the source
of this unseasonable
Storm of passionate regard that would self-
combust for the
Briefest glimpse into the electric warmth of
your own heart,
Smiling through the lovely dark-brown
mirrors of your
Soul! Like the thirsty Earth, I seek my
consort from the
Elemental pillars that support the infinite
skies
and taunt the sighs of heaven itself!

THE BATTLE

Tweedledum and Tweedledee
Decided to go to war,
For Tweedledum said Tweedledee
Had made him really sore!

Each intent on wreaking woe
They bravely fumed and sassed,
But Tweedledee had dined on beans
And Tweedledum got gassed!

(Jotted on an envelope while SCUDS flew overhead, Riyadh 1991)

123

VECTOR TO THE TARGET

I am with you as the pilot is with the silver
projectile he flies,
Merging his flesh and bone to steel and
white-hot flame
As he enters his cocoon of protective
complexity and life support
To initiate the measured process of bringing
the stored potential of his
Fantastic machine to life, furious energy to
the furnaces of its massive
Engines, whining electric activity to its
artificial intelligence, and
Coursing, life-giving fluidic circulation to
the vital hydraulics of its core.
Once on the ramp, the pilot guides the
straining craft towards its mark,
Pausing to run up the screaming engines
while awaiting clearance. A final
Check and throttles ram forward to full
reheat, the great machine leaping
Like a hungry bird of prey for the freedom
of azure skies that wait beyond,
Its power fully unleashed in twin
maelstroms of screaming combustion
So too would I enter your female plexus,
merge myself within
Your molten core of sensual yin, connecting
with dormant fires of
Spiritual force, smoldering blood, soul, and
body that is Sukiko the lover and instructor.

So also would I slowly bring your dormant
body to electric life, restoring heat to
Your arctic polar core, and feeling to your
dulled thresholds of sensate life.
And then, as we paused on the farthest edge
of your now awakened sensitivities,
I would plunge myself deeply into full
forward thrust, pushing your resistance back
Into the cushions with the spooled-up
accelerations of my desire, flying you off
This earth into the most rare and delicious
heavens of compressed coital heat
On powerful wings of human sinew and
straining muscle, filling your recesses,
Reaching for space to bear you, pinioned
and transfixed, across the brilliant
Explosive purple skies of sensory ecstasies,
as we soar like *Tsuru* of the Dawn
Upon the urgent vector of my physical
desire for all that are, in the perfect
Loveliness of your womanly warrior form...a
vector to the target of your life
That consumes me with recurring passion.
The steel warhead in the velvet missile
Awakened at long last
and on its way to
the target...

J'AI EU UNE MERDE SAINE...

Sometimes life is like that. A simple healthy shit,
A cup of black coffee, a good loaf of French bread,
Wine and cheese under a cool oak tree in the park.

Sometimes life is right there. Unexpected,
Uncomplicated and flowing along like a strong river current
Under the hot sun of a lazy afternoon.

Sometimes it's good to simply *feel* and
Switch off the thinking, reach out for the big breast of life
That is offered to suckle with innocent joy.

Sometimes it is better to mate and roll and writhe
On God's green grass with abandon, before the heat of coupling
Spreads its brush fire too wildly among the weeds of life.

Sometimes it's all the time. Sometimes it's not.
Sometimes the importance of all the heaped up daily *merde*
We experience isn't worth a good, satisfying fart!

Sometimes there's just no time left in the

world
To quickly question all the good feelings that
spring briefly
Out of the waters of our lives, like ghostly
silver trout at dusk

Sometimes that brief flash of insight that
presents
Without a price and negotiates tranquility is
better caught
And held and marveled at without question
or second guess.

Sometimes it is ours to delight, sometimes
not, but always
Ours to bemoan and deny. And sometimes it
is ours to know
How and when the two diverge, before the
magic moment flees.

Sometimes it really *is*, sometimes...like a
healthy shit,
A satisfying fuck, an amusing thought.
Sometimes life is like that.
Sometimes life with you, *sometimes*...

About the Author

Kalikiano Kalei lives in Sacramento CA, with his wife, several Husky dogs, and a Convair F-106A *'Delta Dart'* (59-0010) that he is very 'attached' to (image taken in 2016).

CPSIA information can be obtained
at www.ICGtesting.com
Printed in the USA
BVOW06*0404240817
492935BV00002B/3/P